My Life ▪
in Black and White

Copyright © 2007 by Anotei M. Baatz

All rights reserved. This book or parts thereof, may not be reproduced in any form without permission. Your support of the Author's rights is appreciated.

To order additional copies, please go to www.lulu.com/anotei
Or email Anotei directly at anotei@gmail.com

ISBN: 978-0-6151-3967-8

Printed by Lulu.com

Table of Contents

Welcome	7
Journal Layout	8
Helpful Tips	9
Introduction	11
The First Years	12
My Childhood	18
Free Flow ▪ Free Flow ▪ Free Flow	25
My Family ▪ The Parents	27
My Family ▪ The Siblings	35
My Family ▪ The Children	39
My Family ▪ Traditions	43
My Family	44
My Family ▪ The Grandparents	45
My Family ▪ Aunts, Uncles and Cousins	53
My Family ▪ Unofficial Members	57
Essay	61
My Favorites ▪ The Foods	63
My Favorites ▪ The Drinks	64
Free Flow ▪ Free Flow ▪ Free Flow	65
My Thoughts On	67
Essay	69
Me Physically	71
Just for Today	74
Core Values	79
Essay	82
Survey	83
Free Flow ▪ Free Flow ▪ Free Flow	84
My Thoughts On	86
School Years – Elementary	88
School Years – Middle School	95
School Years – College Or Trade	103
The Favorites – Written Things	115
Free Flow ▪ Free Flow ▪ Free Flow	116
My Favorites ▪ The Places	118
Just for Today	119
Transportation – The Automobile	124
My Thoughts On	129
Essay	131
Survey	133
Free Flow ▪ Free Flow ▪ Free Flow	134
Geography	136
Essay	143
My Thoughts On	145
Hobbies	147

Friends	149
Love	157
My Current Lover	169
Past Lovers	171
Just for Today	186
Free Flow ▪ Free Flow ▪ Free Flow	191
Essay	193
The Favorites - Nature	194
Careers	195
Free Flow ▪ Free Flow ▪ Free Flow	205
My Thoughts On	207
Survey	209
Essay	210
Survey	212
Personal Philosophy	213
Essay	220
Survey	222
Influential People	223
Free Flow ▪ Free Flow ▪ Free Flow	229
Defining Moments	231
Current Pets	245
Past Pets	246
Just for Today	249
Music	254
Sports	255
My Favorites – The Games	256
Religion	257
Politics	260
Talents	261
Mystery Things	263
Free Flow ▪ Free Flow ▪ Free Flow	266
My Favorites – The Movies	268
The Favorites – Television	272
What If	273
Fears	275
Medical Facts	276
In the End	277
Free Flow ▪ Free Flow ▪ Free Flow	280
Pet Peeves	282
Where Was I When	283
Almost Famous	287
Simple Pleasures	288
Fads and Fashion	289
Essay	290
Final Thoughts	295
Guest Writer	300
Continuation Pages	316

Welcome

I believe <u>every life</u> is an interesting story that should be remembered and shared.

I arrived at the idea for a prompted journal after receiving a chain e-mail asking me some random questions. I thought, what a neat idea. I'd love to do something similar which would summarize interesting facts about me, my experiences and my life. Every year, typically around the New Year, I attempt to keep a journal. I have failed miserably in my attempts. So the idea for this journal was born from my desire to have a journal, but one that maybe didn't require so much self-directed inspiration on my part.

This journal is designed to help those of us with good intentions, but limited time. The journal includes short chapters where you simply fill in the blanks. There are miscellaneous quizzes for you to complete and there are a few thought-provoking essay questions.

Not every topic will apply to you and you may find some obvious topics missing. For example, I excluded marriage and instead have a section on love. I've included free flow pages for you to add things you wish to add.

I hope this format will allow you to jot down ideas, thoughts and important values about your life. I also hope this journal will become a keepsake for you and your loved ones to read and reread for many years to come.

Happy Journaling ▪

Anotei

Journal Layout

- CHAPTERS – themed questions typically covering one topic
- FREE FLOW – blank pages to write about any topic you choose
- ESSAYS – random, thought provoking questions
- SURVEY – short, multiple-choice questions
- JUST TODAY – questions based on the day you're completing the section
- MY THOUGHTS ON – controversial issues
- FAVORITES – just fill-in the blanks
- WHAT IF – poses a hypothetical question for you to answer
- WHERE WERE YOU WHEN – significant events occurred
- GUEST WRITERS – allows you to have others add to your journal

Helpful Tips

- Before starting your journal, flip through the pages to familiarize yourself with the questions and formatting

- Some questions may prompt the same or similar answers, consider making notes in pencil to determine which answers you want under which chapter

- Consider completing the journal in random order; much like your memory which is also a random compilation

- If you run out of writing space, there are pages at the back, numbered for your continuation

Introduction

My Name ▪

This journal is ▪

☐ private ☐ accessible by invitation only

I received this journal ▪

☐ as a gift ☐ bought it for myself

Today's Date ▪

Comments about Today ▪

The First Years

Legal Name ▪

Date of Birth ▪   Birthplace ▪

Time of Birth ▪   Weight and Length ▪

How my parents decided on my name ▪

Other names my parents considered for me ▪

Nicknames and how I earned them ▪

The First Years

What would my name be if I were born the opposite sex ▪

What would my name be if I could choose it ▪

Interesting story about my birth ▪

The First Years

Childhood stories my parents tell again and again ■

The First Years

Childhood stories my parents tell again and again ▪

The First Years

My First Words ▪

I started walking at ▪

Favorite Foods ▪

Favorite Toys ▪

Playmates ▪

The First Years

Free Space ■

My Childhood

I spent a lot of time ▪

My favorite games were ▪

When I grow up, I want to be ▪

My favorite TV shows ▪

My Childhood

My fondest childhood memory ▪

My Childhood

My worst childhood memory ▪

My Childhood

Fears or Phobias I developed as a child ▪

Childhood Traumas ▪

My Childhood

Family Vacations ■

Chores and Allowance ■

My Childhood

When people ask me where I grew up, I say ▪

My Childhood

What social/economic class was your family growing up ▪ how did this affect you in a positive or negative way ▪

Free Flow ▪ Free Flow ▪ Free Flow

Free Flow ▪ Free Flow ▪ Free Flow

My Family ▪ The Parents

Mother's Name ▪

Current Age ▪   Birthday ▪

Father's Name ▪

Current Age ▪   Birthday ▪

How did they meet ▪

My Family • The Parents

Valuable lessons my parents taught me •

My Family • The Parents

Valuable lessons my parents taught me ▪

My Family ▪ The Parents

Valuable lessons my parents taught me ▪

Fond memories of my parents ▪

My Family ▪ The Parents

Fond memories of my parents ▪

My Family • The Parents

Not so fond memories of my parents ▪

My Family • The Parents

Not so fond memories of my parents ▪

My Family ▪ The Siblings

Names and Ages ▪

How I am similar to my siblings ▪

My Family ▪ The Siblings

How I differ from my siblings ▪

My Family • The Siblings

Do you have a favorite sibling •

My Family ▪ The Siblings

Fond memories growing up with my siblings ▪

My Family ▪ The Children

Name ▪   Age ▪

What makes this child special ▪

My Family ▪ The Children

Name ▪   Age ▪

What makes this child special ▪

My Family ▪ The Children

Name ▪   Age ▪

What makes this child special ▪

My Family ▪ The Children

Name ▪   Age ▪

What makes this child special ▪

My Family ▪ Traditions

Family Traditions ▪

My Family

Things that make my family special ▪

My Family ▪ The Grandparents

Grandmother's Name ▪

Grandfather's Name ▪

How did they meet ▪

My Family ▪ The Grandparents

Fond memories of my Grandparents ▪

My Family • The Grandparents

Fond memories of my Grandparents •

My Family • The Grandparents

Fond memories of my Grandparents •

My Family ▪ The Grandparents

Fond memories of my Grandparents ▪

My Family ▪ The Grandparents

Not so fond memories of your Grandparents ▪

My Family — The Grandparents

Not so fond memories of your Grandparents ▪

My Family ▪ The Grandparents

Not so fond memories of your Grandparents ▪

My Family ▪ Aunts, Uncles and Cousins

Favorite Aunts or Uncles ▪

My Family • Aunts, Uncles and Cousins

Favorite Aunts or Uncles ▪

My Family • Aunts, Uncles and Cousins

Favorite Cousins •

My Family • Aunts, Uncles and Cousins

Favorite Cousins •

My Family ▪ Unofficial Members

Name and why they are important ▪

My Family • Unofficial Members

Name and why they are important •

My Family ▪ Unofficial Members

Name and why they are important ▪

My Family • Unofficial Members

Name and why they are important •

Essay

Things you believed as a child that you later learned were not accurate ▪

Essay

Things you believed as a child that you later learned were not accurate ▪

My Favorites ▪ The Foods

Bread ▪

Breakfast ▪

Cereal ▪

Cheese ▪

Dessert ▪

Dinner ▪

Fruit ▪

Lunch ▪

Meat ▪

Nuts ▪

Pizza ▪

Salad ▪

Sandwich ▪

Seafood ▪

Soup ▪

Vegetable ▪

Other Favorites ▪

My Favorites ▪ The Drinks

Beer ▪

Wine ▪

Cocktail ▪

Soft Drink ▪

Juice ▪

Other ▪

Other Favorites ▪

Free Flow ▪ Free Flow ▪ Free Flow

Free Flow ■ Free Flow ■ Free Flow

My Thoughts On

The Disciplining of Children ▪

My Thoughts On

The Disciplining of Children ▪

Essay

If you witnessed a parent being verbally abusive or striking their child, what would you do?

Essay

If you witnessed a parent being verbally abusive or striking their child, what would you do?

Me Physically

- Height
- Eye Color
- Hair Color
- Shoes Size
- Shirt Size
- Best Physical Traits

- Weight
- Eyewear
- Length and texture
- Pant Size

- Worst Physical Traits

Me Physically

One thing I would change about my physical make-up ▪

Good Habits ▪

Bad Habits ▪

Me Physically

Tattoos ▪

Piercing ▪

Right-Handed, Left-Handed or Both ▪

Ticklish ▪ Where ▪

Can I roll my R's ▪

Birthmarks ▪

Just for Today

Today's date and day ▪

My current age ▪

Where am I ▪

What am I wearing ▪

Last thing I ate ▪

Last person I spoke to ▪

Just for Today

What did we discuss ▪

What did I do with my day ▪

Just for Today

Last TV show I watched ▪

Last movie I saw ▪

Last song I heard ▪

School, Working, Retired? ▪

Just for Today

Current Friends ▪

Current Love ▪

Just for Today

My current attitude is ▪

Core Values

Pick your top three Core Values and explain why they are important to you

Authenticity	Fame	Family	Happiness	Influence
Integrity	Joy	Justice	Love	Peace
Power	Recognition	Status	Success	Friendship
Truth	Wealth	Wisdom		

Other_____

Core Value #1.

Core Values

Core Value #2.

Core Values

Core Value #3.

Essay

Describe your bedroom ▪

Survey

I believe in ▪ ▪ ▪

	Yes	Sometimes	No
100% honesty	☐	☐	☐
Angels	☐	☐	☐
Demonic Possession	☐	☐	☐
Easter Bunny	☐	☐	☐
Evolution	☐	☐	☐
Fairy Tales/Fairies	☐	☐	☐
Fate/Destiny	☐	☐	☐
Ghosts	☐	☐	☐
God	☐	☐	☐
Gypsies	☐	☐	☐
Horoscopes	☐	☐	☐
Karma	☐	☐	☐
Leprechauns	☐	☐	☐
Life after death	☐	☐	☐
Life on other planets	☐	☐	☐
Love at first sight	☐	☐	☐
Monsters	☐	☐	☐
Pirates	☐	☐	☐
Revenge	☐	☐	☐
Santa Claus	☐	☐	☐
Vampires	☐	☐	☐

Free Flow ▪ Free Flow ▪ Free Flow

Free Flow ▪ Free Flow ▪ Free Flow

My Thoughts On

Racism ▪

My Thoughts On

Racism ▪

School Years – Elementary

Name of Elementary School(s) ▪

Favorite Teachers ▪

Favorite Subjects ▪

Friends ▪

School Years — Elementary

Special Projects ▪

Awards and Honors ▪

School Years — Elementary

Childhood Crushes ▪

School Years – Elementary

Fond Memories ▪

School Years – Elementary

Fond Memories ▪

School Years – Elementary

Not so Fond Memories ▪

School Years – Elementary

Not so Fond Memories ▪

School Years – Middle School

Name of Middle School(s) ▪

Favorite Teachers ▪

Favorite Subjects ▪

Friends ▪

School Years – Middle School

Clubs ▪

Controversy ▪

School Years — Middle School

Special Projects ▪

Awards and Honors ▪

School Years – Middle School

Young Crushes ▪

School Years – Middle School

Fond Memories ▪

School Years – Middle School

Fond Memories ▪

School Years – Middle School

Not so Fond Memories ▪

School Years — Middle School

Not so Fond Memories ▪

School Years – College Or Trade

Name of School(s) ▪

Favorite Instructors ▪

Favorite Courses ▪

SCHOOL YEARS – College Or Trade

Friends ▪

SCHOOL YEARS – College Or Trade

Special Projects ▪

Awards and Honors ▪

SCHOOL YEARS — College Or Trade

Clubs, Fraternities, and/or Sororities ▪

SCHOOL YEARS — College Or Trade

Fond Memories ▪

SCHOOL YEARS – College Or Trade

Fond Memories ▪

SCHOOL YEARS – College Or Trade

Not so Fond Memories ▪

SCHOOL YEARS – College Or Trade

Not so Fond Memories ▪

SCHOOL YEARS — College Or Trade

Controversial Issues ▪

SCHOOL YEARS – College Or Trade

Controversial Issues ▪

SCHOOL YEARS – College Or Trade

Controversial Issues ▪

SCHOOL YEARS — College Or Trade

Controversial Issues ▪

The Favorites – Written Things

Favorite Books ▪

Favorite Authors ▪

Newspaper ▪

Magazine ▪

Comic Strip ▪

Book You're Reading Now ▪

Last Book You Really Enjoyed ▪

Free Flow ▪ Free Flow ▪ Free Flow

Free Flow ▪ Free Flow ▪ Free Flow

My Favorites ▪ The Places

City ▪

Country ▪

Restaurant ▪

Store ▪

Place to meet friends ▪

Just for Today

Today's date and day ▪

My current age ▪

Where am I ▪

What am I wearing ▪

Last thing I ate ▪

Last person I spoke to ▪

Just for Today

What did we discuss ▪

What did I do with my day ▪

Just for Today

Last TV show I watched ▪

Last movie I saw ▪

Last song I heard ▪

School, Working, Retired? ▪

Just for Today

Current Friends ▪

Current Love ▪

Just for Today

Last person I spoke to on the phone ▪

My current attitude is ▪

Transportation – The Automobile

First Car ▪ ▪ ▪ Year, Make and Model ▪

First Car that I paid for: Year, Make and Model ▪

Who taught me how to drive ▪

How many times did I fail my driver's test ▪

Can I drive a manual transmission ▪

Transportation – The Automobile

Dream Car ▪

Traffic Tickets ▪

Suffer from road rage ▪

Ever in a car accident ▪

Transportation – The Motorcycle

Love or Hate them ▪

Driver, Rider or Both ▪

Other thoughts on Motorcycles ▪

Transportation – The Airplane

The first time I ever flew ▪

My destination ▪

How I feel about flying ▪

Transportation – Any Other

Trains, Subways, Boats, Hot Air Balloons, Other ▪

My Thoughts On

Abortion ▪

MY THOUGHTS ON

Abortion ▪

Essay

My house is on fire, what three things do I make sure I take ▪

Essay

Your house is on fire, what three things do I make sure I take ∎

Survey

If I have to choose, I choose ▪ ▪ ▪

CHOCOLATE	VANILLA
PRO-LIFE	PRO-CHOICE
REGULAR	DECAFINATED
SWEET	SOUR
CAR	TRUCK
TELEVISION	MOVIES
NAUGHTY	NICE
LIFE IN PRISON	DEATH PENALTY
READ	WRITE
LISTEN	TALK
EARLY TO BED	LATE TO BED
RAIN	SUN
WALK	RUN
KISSES	HUGS
WITH NUTS	WITHOUT NUTS

Free Flow ▪ Free Flow ▪ Free Flow

Free Flow • Free Flow • Free Flow

Geography

Places I have lived ▪

Geography

Places I have visited ▪

Geography

First time I saw the ocean ▪

Geography

Places I'd like to visit ▪

Geography

Great Vacations ▪

Great Vacations ■

Geography

Geography

Great Vacations ▪

Essay

If money were no object, I would live ▪

Essay

If money were no object, I would live ▪

My Thoughts On

The Environment and Global Warming ▪

My Thoughts On

The Environment and Global Warming

Hobbies

My Hobbies ■

Hobbies

What types of things do I like to do in my free time ▪

Friends

Best Friends ▪

Friends

Oldest Friend ■

Friends

Dearest Friend

Friends

Characteristics I value in my friends ▪

Friends

A friend you love, but secretly hate ▪

Friends

Friendships that have ended ▪ and why ▪

Friendships that have ended ▪ and why ▪

Friends

Friendships that have ended ▪ and why ▪

First Date ▪ **Love**

Love

Best Date ▪

Love

Worst Date ▪

Love

Love Letters Written ▪

Love Letters Received ▪

Love

First Kiss ▪

Love

Greatest Kiss ▪

Love

First Sexual Experience ▪

First Sexual Experience ▪

First True Love ▪

Last True Love ▪

Love

A description of my ideal mate ▪

My Current Lover

Name ▪

How we met ▪

What I love most about this person ▪

My Current Lover

Their best traits ▪

How did we fall in love ▪

Past Lovers

Name ▪

How long did we date ▪

How we met ▪

Past Lovers

Positives about this love ▪

Negatives about this love ▪

Past Lovers

Why we aren't together ▪

Where is this person now ▪

Past Lovers

Name ▪

How long did we date ▪

How we met ▪

Past Lovers

Positives about this love ▪

Negatives about this love ▪

Past Lovers

Why we aren't together ▪

Where is this person now ▪

Past Lovers

Name ▪

How long did we date ▪

How we met ▪

Past Lovers

Positives about this love ▪

Negatives about this love ▪

Past Lovers

Why we aren't together ▪

Where is this person now ▪

Past Lovers

Name ▪

How long did we date ▪

How we met ▪

Past Lovers

Positives about this love ▪

Negatives about this love ▪

Past Lovers

Why we aren't together ▪

Where is this person now ▪

Past Lovers

Name ▪

How long did we date ▪

How we met ▪

Past Lovers

Positives about this love ▪

Negatives about this love ▪

Past Lovers

Why we aren't together ▪

Where is this person now ▪

Just for Today

Today's date and day ▪

My current age ▪

Where am I ▪

What am I wearing ▪

Last thing I ate ▪

Last person I spoke to ▪

Just for Today

What did we discuss ▪

What did I do with my day ▪

Just for Today

Last TV show I watched ▪

Last movie I saw ▪

Last song I heard ▪

School, Working, Retired? ▪

Just for Today

Current Friends ▪

Current Love ▪

Just for Today

My current attitude is ▪

Free Flow ▪ Free Flow ▪ Free Flow

Free Flow ▪ Free Flow ▪ Free Flow

Essay

Are there any past loves that you think about on a constant basis ∎

The Favorites - Nature

NATURE ■ ■ ■

Flower ■   Tree ■

Season ■   Weather ■

THE SENSES ■ ■ ■

Sound ■   Sight ■

Smell ■   Feeling ■

Taste ■

TIME ■ ■ ■

Time of Day ■   Day of Week ■

Holiday ■   Age ■

Careers

My First Job ▪

How did I get my first job ▪

What did I like about my first job ▪

What did I hate about my first job ▪

Careers

My other various jobs ■

Careers

My most rewarding job ■

Careers

How I chose my career ▪

Careers

Memorable Co-Workers ▪

Careers

My Best Boss ▪

Careers

My Worst Boss ■

Careers

Sticky Work Situations ▪

Careers

Sticky Work Situations ■

Careers

Retirement Dream(s) ▪

Free Flow ▪ Free Flow ▪ Free Flow

Free Flow ■ Free Flow ■ Free Flow

My Thoughts On

Homosexuality ▪

My Thoughts On

Homosexuality ▪

Survey

	LOVE 'EM	JUST OK	HATE 'EM
Babies	☐	☐	☐
Dogs	☐	☐	☐
Cats	☐	☐	☐
Sushi	☐	☐	☐
Broccoli	☐	☐	☐
Tomatoes	☐	☐	☐
Jell-O	☐	☐	☐
Fruit Cake	☐	☐	☐
Popcorn	☐	☐	☐
Tequila	☐	☐	☐
Oysters	☐	☐	☐
Gyros	☐	☐	☐
Funnel Cake	☐	☐	☐
Watermelon	☐	☐	☐
Asparagus	☐	☐	☐
Cottage Cheese	☐	☐	☐
Sour Cream	☐	☐	☐
Coffee	☐	☐	☐
Pickles	☐	☐	☐
Black Olives	☐	☐	☐
Green Olives	☐	☐	☐
Haunted Houses	☐	☐	☐

Essay

You are told you have a week to live, how do you spend your week ■

Essay

You are told you have a week to live, how do you spend your week ■

Survey

Bite your fingernails	Yes	No
Cheated on a Test	Yes	No
Chinese Fire Drill	Yes	No
Drink Alcohol	Yes	No
Drink and Drive	Yes	No
Premarital sex	Yes	No
Served in the Military	Yes	No
Sing in the shower	Yes	No
Sing to the radio	Yes	No
Smoke	Yes	No
Steal Merchandise	Yes	No
Steal Money	Yes	No
Used a Fake ID	Yes	No
Voted	Yes	No

Personal Philosophy

The things that I am passionate about ▪

Personal Philosophy

The things that I am passionate about ▪

Personal Philosophy

My Mantras ▪

Personal Philosophy

My Mantras ▪

Personal Philosophy

My Favorite Sayings ▪

My Favorite Bumper Sticker ▪

Personal Philosophy

My Hopes and Dreams ▪

Personal Philosophy

Personal Theories ▪

Essay

If you witnessed a man being verbally abusive to a woman, and she looked very frightened what would you do ▪

Essay

If you witnessed a woman being verbally abusive to a man, and he looked very frightened what would you do ▪

Survey

	Yes	I might	Only If I have To	No Way
Bungee Jump	☐	☐	☐	☐
Dined and Dash	☐	☐	☐	☐
Eat a Bug	☐	☐	☐	☐
Parachute	☐	☐	☐	☐
Shave my head	☐	☐	☐	☐
Streak	☐	☐	☐	☐

Any desire to explain yourself ▪

Influential People

This person has made a difference in my life ▪

Influential People

This person has made a difference in my life ▪

Influential People

This person has made a difference in my life ▪

Influential People

This person has made a difference in my life ▪

Influential People

This person has made a difference in my life ▪

Influential People

This person has made a difference in my life ▪

Free Flow ▪ Free Flow ▪ Free Flow

Free Flow • Free Flow • Free Flow

Defining Moments

This moment is etched in my memory as changing the course of my life, or how I choose to live it ▪

Defining Moments

This moment is etched in my memory as changing the course of my life, or how I choose to live it ▪

Defining Moments

This moment is etched in my memory as changing the course of my life, or how I choose to live it ▪

Defining Moments

This moment is etched in my memory as changing the course of my life, or how I choose to live it ▪

Defining Moments

This moment is etched in my memory as changing the course of my life, or how I choose to live it ▪

Defining Moments

The nicest thing I have ever done for someone ■

Defining Moments

The nicest thing someone has ever done for me ▪

Defining Moments

The best gift I've ever received ▪

Defining Moments

The best compliment I've ever received ▪

Defining Moments

The best compliment I've ever received ▪

Defining Moments

List any song that triggers a memory and describe the memory ▪

Defining Moments

List any song that triggers a memory and describe the memory ▪

Defining Moments

Describe a time when you felt the most loved ▪

Defining Moments

Describe a time when you felt the most loved ▪

Current Pets

Name and type ▪

Characteristics ▪

Tricks ▪

How did this pet come to live with you ▪

Fondest Memory ▪

Past Pets

Name and type ▪

Characteristics ▪

Tricks ▪

How did you get this pet ▪

How long did they live ▪

What happened to them ▪

Fondest Memory ▪

Past Pets

Name and type ▪

Characteristics ▪

Tricks ▪

How did you get this pet ▪

How long did they live ▪

What happened to them ▪

Fondest Memory ▪

Past Pets

Name and type ▪

Characteristics ▪

Tricks ▪

How did you get this pet ▪

How long did they live ▪

What happened to them ▪

Fondest Memory ▪

Just for Today

Today's date and day ▪

My current age ▪

Where am I ▪

What am I wearing ▪

Last thing I ate ▪

Last person I spoke to ▪

Just for Today

What did we discuss ▪

What did I do with my day ▪

Just for Today

Last TV show I watched ▪

Last movie I saw ▪

Last song I heard ▪

School, Working, Retired? ▪

Just for Today

Current Friends ▪

Current Love ▪

Just for Today

My current attitude is ▪

Music

Favorite type of music ▪

Favorite Bands ▪

Singers ▪

Songs ▪

Sports

Favorite Sports to Watch ▪

Favorite Sports to Play ▪

My Favorites – The Games

Card Games ▪

Board Games ▪

Word Games ▪

Casino Games ▪

Video Games ▪

Online/Computer Games ▪

Dice Games ▪

Religion

Thoughts on God ▪

Religion

Thoughts on God ▪

Religion

Religious Beliefs ▪

Politics

Political Affiliation ▪

The last time I voted, I voted for ▪

Talents

My talents are ▪

Talents

I've received the following rewards and/or recognition for my talent ▪

Unknown Facts ▪ **Mystery Things**

Mystery Things

Things people would not guess about me ▪

Weird Talents ■

Free Flow ▪ Free Flow ▪ Free Flow

Free Flow ▪ Free Flow ▪ Free Flow

My Favorites – The Movies

Drama ▪

Action ▪

Comedy ▪

Horror ▪

Science-Fiction ▪

Other ▪

Animation ▪

Celebrity

Top Five Celebrities you'd like to meet ▪

Celebrity

Female Celebrity you admire most ▪

Male Celebrity you admire most ▪

Famous People I saw in person ▪

Famous People I actually had a conversation with ▪

Celebrity

The Favorites – Television

Drama ▪

Comedy ▪

Game Show ▪

Reality TV ▪

Talk Show ▪

News Program ▪

Cartoon ▪

Channel ▪

Actor(s) ▪

Actress(es) ▪

What If

If you could meet any historical figure, who would you like to meet ▪

What If

If you could meet any relative that has died, who would you meet ▪

Fears

I have a fear of ▪

Medical Facts

Blood Type ▪

Things I've had ▪

Ever Hospitalized ▪

Ever Broken a Bone ▪

Ever had Stitches ▪

In the End

When I die, I wish for the following ▪

In the End

When I die, I wish for the following for my remains ▪

Am I an organ donor ▪

In the End

My other wishes ▪

Free Flow ▪ Free Flow ▪ Free Flow

Free Flow • Free Flow • Free Flow

Pet Peeves

A few of my pet peeves are ▪

Where Was I When

Space Shuttle Challenger January 28, 1986 ▪

Where Was I When

Princess Diana Died August 31, 1997 ▪

Where Was I When

World Trade Center Bombing September 11, 2001 ▪

Where Was I When

Saddam Hussein Executed December 29, 2006 ▪

Almost Famous

I have been on ▪

TV, the Radio, in the Newspaper, in a Movie, in a Play, in a Concert ▪ ▪ ▪

Simple Pleasures

My simple pleasures are ▪

Fads and Fashion

My thoughts on Fashion ▪

Fads during my lifetime ▪

Essay

These are the things that make me feel rich ▪

Essay

These are the things that make me feel rich ▪

Essay

My attitudes and thoughts about money ■

Essay

My attitudes and thoughts about money ▪

Essay

Words people use to describe me ▪

Final Thoughts

Final Thoughts

Final Thoughts

Final Thoughts

Final Thoughts

Guest Writer

Guest Writer

Guest Writer

Guest Writer

Guest Writer

Guest Writer

Guest Writer

Guest Writer

Guest Writer

Guest Writer

Guest Writer

Guest Writer

Guest Writer

Guest Writer

Guest Writer

Guest Writer

Continuation Pages

Continuation Pages

Continuation Pages

Continuation Pages

Continuation Pages

Continuation Pages

Continuation Pages

Continuation Pages

Continuation Pages

Continuation Pages

Continuation Pages

Continuation Pages

Continuation Pages

Continuation Pages

Continuation Pages

Continuation Pages

Continuation Pages

Continuation Pages

Continuation Pages

Continuation Pages

Continuation Pages

Continuation Pages

Continuation Pages

Continuation Pages

Continuation Pages

Continuation Pages

Continuation Pages

Continuation Pages

Continuation Pages

Continuation Pages

Continuation Pages

Continuation Pages

Continuation Pages

Continuation Pages

Continuation Pages

Continuation Pages

Continuation Pages

Continuation Pages

Continuation Pages

Continuation Pages

Continuation Pages

www.ingramcontent.com/pod-product-compliance
Lightning Source LLC
Chambersburg PA
CBHW080330170426
43194CB00014B/2515